NO. **5**

UNIVERSITY OF MINNESOTA PAMPHLETS
ON AMERICAN WRITERS   65 CENTS

Mark Twain

BY LEWIS LEARY

UNIVERSITY OF MINNESOTA

Mark Twain

BY LEWIS LEARY

UNIVERSITY OF MINNESOTA PRESS • MINNEAPOLIS

Printed in the United States of America at the North Central
Publishing Company, St. Paul

Library of Congress Catalog Card Number: 60–62856

PUBLISHED IN GREAT BRITAIN, INDIA, AND PAKISTAN BY THE OXFORD
UNIVERSITY PRESS, LONDON, BOMBAY, AND KARACHI, AND IN
CANADA BY THOMAS ALLEN, LTD., TORONTO

MARK TWAIN

LEWIS LEARY, a professor of English at Columbia University, is the author or editor of a number of books on American literature, including *That Rascal Freneau, The Literary Career of Nathaniel Tucker,* and *Contemporary Literary Scholarship.*

⤏ *Mark Twain*

Mᴏsᴛ Aᴍᴇʀɪᴄᴀɴs regard Mark Twain with special affection. They know him as a shaggy man who told stories of boy adventures so much like their own or those they would like to have had that they become intimately a part of personal experience. His cheerful irreverence and unhurried pace seem antidotes for attitudes to which they necessarily but unwillingly surrender. His is the image of what they like to think Americans have been or can be: humorously perceptive, undeceived by sham, successful in spite of circumstance because of distinctive personal characteristics.

More often than not they smile approvingly at his portrayal of man as "a museum of diseases, a home of impurities," who "begins as dirt and departs as stench," created for no apparent purpose except the nourishment and entertainment of microbes. The words seem bold and appropriately bitter, iconoclastically vulgar but, for all of that, funny. Evolution failed when man appeared, for his is the only bad heart in all the animal kingdom; only he is capable of malice, vindictiveness, drunkenness; when he is not cruel, he is stupid, like a sheep. It does seem such a pity, commented Mark Twain, that Noah and his companions did not miss their boat. And he tempts readers toward the compulsive nightmare of our time by wondering if a device might not be invented which could exterminate man by withdrawing all oxygen from the air for two minutes.

They admire Mark Twain's hardheaded exposures of human venality, but respond also to his unembarrassed sentiment, his compassion and simple humility. What any man sees in the human race, he once admitted, "is merely himself in the deep and private

honesty of his own heart." Everything human is pathetic: "The secret source of Humor itself is not joy but sorrow. There is no humor in heaven." He would have agreed with Robert Frost that earth is the right place for love, but would have added that it is inevitably also the place for stumbling and then forgetting the hurt by recalling or inventing other, older, and less disreputable times.

No wonder then that Ernest Hemingway found all American literature to begin with Mark Twain. His escape to adventure, to the past, to humor which moves through and beyond reality, is not unlike Hemingway's escape from thinking through the simpler pleasures of wine, women, and manly exercise. Not only is Mark Twain's simple declarative style a parent of Hemingway's style; not only is his boy's-eye view of the world like Hemingway's view, like Willa Cather's, Sherwood Anderson's, even J. D. Salinger's; the publication of *The Mysterious Stranger* in 1916 reveals him mastered by the same cluster of opinions which produced the retreat to older times of Henry Adams, as well as the despair of the "lost generation" of Hemingway and Scott Fitzgerald, and the wasted land of T. S. Eliot.

It was as difficult to convince people of his time as it is to convince people of ours that Mark Twain never really existed except as a character, costumed and carefully rehearsed, cannily a crowd-pleaser. For in both a literary and psychological sense the shambling but perceptive humorist remembered as Mark Twain is a mask, a controlled, drawling, and whimsical voice, a posturing and flamboyant figure, behind which exists the man, Samuel Langhorne Clemens, who with the help of circumstance and receptive wit created him. The image is partly self-portrait, but shrewdly retouched until the character who is Mark Twain becomes Clemens's most successful achievement, and the voice of Mark Twain speaks in a special literary relation to its creator.

6

It is probably true that the two became as confused in Clemens's mind as they have in the minds of people who have talked about Mark Twain, but the distinction is radical. Which is which or who did what to whom remains an important critical puzzle. To simplify more than is appropriate, it can be suggested that Mark Twain was a character who inserted himself, sometimes with joyous abandon, into almost everything which Samuel Clemens wrote. He was irrepressible but self-conscious, alert to his responsibilities as diagnostic spokesman for his time and as representative of much which wove itself into the pattern of contemporary notions of success. But failure to remember that Mark Twain was a medium through whom stories were told, and that he was only in an indirect sense their author, is to fall into the attractively baited trap which opens even more invitingly before commentators on such other American writers as Whitman, Thoreau, and Hemingway, whose masks are more subtle and less clearly designated.

Which spoke when cannot always be determined, nor is the distinction in every case important, except that in some of the writings, and many of them the best, the burden of being Mark Twain is discarded and a voice speaks directly, undistorted by comic pose or anger. Either could have admitted, as one of them did, that his books were like water and the books of great geniuses like wine, but it was surely Mark Twain who supplied the twister to remind us that "everyone drinks water." Part of his character was that of a man among litterateurs, a journalist who detested, he said, novels and poetry, but who liked history, biography, curious facts, and strange happenings.

But it has not been necessary for Americans to read Mark Twain in order to remember him with affection. Probably more people know of Tom Sawyer's slick method of getting a fence whitewashed than have read the book in which it appears. Hollywood versions

of Tom and Huck, of the prince who became a pauper, or of the Yankee from Connecticut who brought American know-how to King Arthur's court have reached millions of viewers, as originally filmed or as adapted for television. A popular comedian has danced and sung his way through a celluloid Camelot. A spectacular Negro boxer has played the runaway slave whose simple loyalty confuses, then converts, Huck Finn. Tom Sawyer has tripped barefooted through a musical comedy, and plans are considered for a musical adaptation of *Innocents Abroad.* More than one actor has found it profitable to dress and drawl as Mark Twain did, and to hold an audience laughter-bound by retelling some of the tales he told.

Mark Twain's laconic, soft speech, whimsical understatements, and outrageous exaggerations made him a platform favorite and pampered after-dinner speaker for more than forty years, and his witticisms were passed by word of mouth and faithfully recorded in newspapers. He saw to that, for he was in every best sense a showman who kept himself and his books effectively before the public. His heavy shock of hair, once red, but soon an eye-catching white, made him seem larger than he was, an illusion which it pleased him later in life to reinforce by dressing summer and winter in white serge or flannel. He learned early how to attract and hold attention, and he used the knowledge well. One way or another, he was the best known and most successfully published author of his generation.

He saw to that also, for — within limits — he was the canny businessman he liked to think himself. His lectures sold his books, and his books helped pack his lectures. As a publisher, he took pride in gauging public taste so well that each book supplied a popular demand. Many were not issued until subscription agents throughout the country had sold in advance enough copies to make them surely profitable. And subscription books in the late

nineteenth century were gaudily attractive books, usually handsomely bound and illustrated — the kind almost anyone would be proud to have on his table, particularly when the author had just been or would soon be in town for a lecture.

For these reasons, though not only for these, Mark Twain's books found themselves in a preferred position in thousands of American homes. At the end of the century, he offered a twenty-two-volume Autograph Edition of his works, which found its way into thousands more, and into libraries, even small town and county libraries which could not afford to buy it but received it as a gift when house shelves became crowded or when it was replaced by the new, twenty-five-volume Underwood Edition a few years later. Shortly before Mark Twain's death in 1910 the Author's National Edition began to appear, and then, in the 1920's, the "definitive edition" in thirty-seven volumes. Few authors, perhaps not even Balzac or Dickens, achieved greater shelf space during their lifetime.

Such success has seemed appropriate, for it fit precisely to patterns which Americans have thought peculiarly their own. Mark Twain was a poor boy who by reason of native skill rose to wealth and fame. He was kin to Daniel Boone or Andrew Jackson because he had known the rigors of our frontier. Abraham Lincoln's rise from log cabin to president created a norm of which his career was a verifying variation — indeed, Howells called him the Lincoln of our literature. He had worked with his hands, like Andrew Carnegie, and then had a large house and servants. These things testified to the validity of what Emerson had said of the divine sufficiency of the individual. Here in truth was the powerful, uneducated democratic personality for whom Whitman had called. Mark Twain walked with kings and capitalists, but never lost the common touch. In his mansion at Hartford, his residence

on Fifth Avenue, or his country place at Stormfield, he still remembered old times and old friends.

This popular image was never completely an accurate likeness, but is sufficiently well drawn to remain attractive. Samuel Langhorne Clemens was born on November 30, 1835, on the Missouri frontier, in a straggling log village called Florida, to which his parents had come from their former home among the hills of Tennessee. His father was a local magistrate and small merchant, originally from Virginia, who had studied law in Kentucky and there met and married auburn-haired Jane Lampton, descended from settlers who had followed Daniel Boone across the mountains. One among thousands of Americans who in the early decades of the nineteenth century moved westward to seek opportunities in newly opened lands, John Marshall Clemens did not prosper in the hamlet in which his third son was born, and so, when Samuel was four years old, moved to Hannibal, a larger town with a population of almost five hundred, on the banks of the Mississippi River.

There, beside this river, Samuel Clemens grew through boyhood much as Tom Sawyer did, fascinated by the life which swarmed over its mile-wide surface or which sought refuge or sustenance on its shores. Through this frontier region passed the picturesque, sometimes mendacious or menacing, pilgrims of restlessly expanding America, up or down the river or across it toward the western plains. Young Samuel must have watched, as any boy might, admiringly, but fearfully also. He saw men maimed or killed in waterfront brawls, Negroes chained like animals for transportation to richer slave markets to the south. He had nightmares and walked in his sleep, and always remembered these things, the rude ways and tremendous talk, and the terror.

Better things were remembered also, like giant rafts and trading

scows piled with produce or sweet-smelling timber, coming from or going where a boy could only guess. Gallant river steamers left wake behind in which small boys swimming or in boats could ride excitedly. Below the village lay wooded Holliday Hill, unrivaled for play at Robin Hood or pirate, and near its summit a cave tempted to exploration. Away from its boisterous riverfront, the village was "a heavenly place for a boy," he said, providing immunities and graces which he never forgot: hunting and fishing, a swimming hole, an inevitable graveyard, truant days at Glasscock's Island, and yearnings toward the better freedom of Tom Blankenship, the town drunkard's son, to whom truancy brought no penalties of conscience or recrimination.

But these days were soon over, for when Samuel was twelve years old, his father died, and the boy was apprenticed to local printers, and then — partaking of a tradition which Benjamin Franklin had established a century before — worked as compositor and pressman for his older brother Orion, who managed a not completely successful newspaper in Hannibal. There was room in its pages for humorous features which young Samuel composed, set to type, and printed over the flamboyant signature of "W. Spaminodas Adrastas Blab" and for miscellaneous items which he collected for "Our Assistant's Column." He even ventured verse, addressing one poem over the signature of "Rambler" ambiguously to "Miss Katie in H—l." The appropriation of so time-worn a pseudonym seems less indicative of literary consciousness than descriptive of desire. Samuel Clemens was not yet a rambler, though he wanted to be, for — again like Franklin — he chaffed under the discipline of a brother, or anyone else.

By the time he was seventeen he was able to think of himself as something more than a local writer. In May 1852 "The Dandy Frightening the Squatter" appeared in the *Carpet-Bag*, a sportsman's magazine in Boston, signed "S.L.C." Done in the slapstick

tradition of native humor such as was being written or was soon to be written by pseudonymous favorites like Sam Slick, Orpheus C. Kerr, and Artemus Ward, it anticipates much of the later manner of Mark Twain: it celebrates the laconic shrewdness of the frontiersman; is told with some of the exaggerated flourishes of the western tall tale, seasoned with caricaturing strokes which may have been learned, even indirectly, from Dickens; and is laid in Hannibal on the Mississippi River. Comparison of its tone and language with Nathaniel Hawthorne's *The Blithedale Romance* or Herman Melville's *Pierre*, which also appeared in that year, suggests some of the things which, for better or worse, were happening or about to happen to writing in the United States.

But wanderlust soon hit young Samuel Clemens, so that he became in fact a rambler. At eighteen he left little Hannibal for St. Louis, the largest town in Missouri, where he saved his wages carefully until he could strike out beyond the limits of his western state, to discover whether a young man's fortune might not be more quickly made in larger cities to the east. He traveled first, by steamboat and rail, through Chicago and Buffalo, to New York, where he worked briefly as a job printer, until he moved southward to become a compositor in Philadelphia and later Washington, then again to Philadelphia, then west to Muscatine, Iowa, to set type for his almost equally peripatetic brother. Soon he was back in St. Louis, and then once more, for two years this time, joined his brother, now in Keokuk, Iowa.

Two years, however, was a long time for a rambler to remain in one place, and his fortune certainly was not being made. He spent the winter of 1856–57 in Cincinnati, but this was a way stop, for he had hit on the notion that a young man almost twenty-two might do well and have fun besides exploring opportunities for riches in South America, along the lush banks of the Amazon. So it was that in April 1857 — the date is a turning point — he started

down the Mississippi toward New Orleans, on his first step toward fame. What happened then — his meeting with the veteran steamboat pilot Horace Bixby, his own apprentice pilot days, his four years of life on the Mississippi — has often been told, and never better than by Clemens himself as he later remembered these years and threw about them the color of romance which only made more persuasive the realism of his detail.

But the abortive trip to South America is remembered for other reasons also, for to make it Samuel Clemens entered into a professional engagement of a kind which later would bring him worldwide acclaim. At Keokuk he shaped the first piece of the pattern which would make continued wanderings possible, even profitable, by arranging with the editor of the *Evening Post* that Samuel Clemens, rambler, would supply reports as regularly as possible on what he saw and did on his ramblings. Only three now appeared, probably because Clemens was deep in the more exciting business of learning to pilot a steamboat. Signed "Thomas Jefferson Snodgrass," they were desperately, self-consciously humorous, hardly distinguishable in language or tone from the work of any other journeyman journalist.

Snodgrass was a name always infinitely funny to Clemens. He used it again in writings in California; more than thirty years later in *The American Claimant* he presented two characters, "Zylobalsamum Snodgrass" and "Spinal Meningitis Snodgrass"; and in *Tom Sawyer Abroad* he spoke of the "celebrated author . . . Snodgrass." While steamboating on the Mississippi from 1857 to 1861, a licensed pilot by the spring of 1859, he contributed letters signed "Quintius Curtius Snodgrass" to the New Orleans *Daily Crescent,* and is said also to have written a burlesque of the pontifical river lore which a retired steamboat captain named Isaiah Sellers printed in a New Orleans paper over the signature of "Mark Twain." A favorite but unverifiable tradition insists that

Captain Sellers was so hurt by the ridicule and Samuel Clemens so conscience-stricken at the wound he had given that a few years later the younger man adopted the old captain's pseudonym — which, as everyone knows, is the leadsman's cry to the pilot when water which is safe, but barely safe, lies ahead.

When in 1861 the Civil War cut across the Mississippi so that river traffic from north to south or south to north was no longer possible, steamboating ceased to be a profitable occupation, and Samuel Clemens was without work. He took only a minor part in the war between the states: one not very dependable account suggests that he was detailed for river duty; the New Orleans Snodgrass letters suggest that he had some connection with militia drill in that city; and Mark Twain later delighted readers of the *Atlantic Monthly* with a humorous "Private History of a Campaign That Failed," which tells how he and a few companions formed themselves into an irregular company which searched vainly for a unit of the Confederate Army to which it might become attached. Whatever his service, it was brief and with the rebellious southern forces — a circumstance which is supposed to have made the later northernized Mark Twain extraordinarily circumspect in speaking of it.

In the summer of 1861 Clemens went farther west, with his brother Orion who had been rewarded for activity in Abraham Lincoln's campaign for the presidency by appointment as secretary of the newly opened Nevada Territory. Orion Clemens, never greatly successful, had little money, but brother Samuel, after profitable years as a river pilot, apparently had his pockets full and provided stage fare for both, traveling himself as unpaid secretary to the new secretary of the territory. The story of their journey across the plains and experiences in Carson City is later recounted in *Roughing It*, in which, as Huck Finn said of him on another occasion, "Mr. Mark Twain . . . he told the truth, mainly." Here

we learn of his adventures in staking out timber claims near Lake Tahoe, only carelessly to leave his campfire unattended so that much of the forest went up in flames. He tells of money invested in silver mines, as he and Orion were caught up in a wild seeking for wealth. Once he was a millionaire for ten days when he found a rich mine, but lost it through carelessness again. Stories of Samuel Clemens in Nevada, variously told by himself or by people who knew him, make up a large share of the public image of Mark Twain. A loose, shambling man, with unruly hair, who lounged about the frontier town in corduroys and shirt sleeves, swapping stories and listening to the way men spoke, he was ready, we are told, to take his chance with the best or worst at poker or in wildcat speculation.

Before he had been in Nevada a year, however, he was back at his old trade as a writer for newspapers, contributing burlesque sketches over the signature of "Josh" to the *Territorial Enterprise* in Virginia City. There he lived freely among friends like fiery Steve Gillis, a printer whose escapades were to keep them both in trouble. The unrestraint of that remarkable frontier paper stimulated Clemens to such journalistic hoaxes as "The Petrified Man" and "The Dutch Nick Massacre," which to his joy were copied as true in eastern papers. Here he first met Artemus Ward and spent convivial evenings with the popular humorist, who advised him how Mark Twain — for Clemens was now using that name — might extend his reputation. Already known as the Washoe Giant, the wild humorist of the Sage Brush Hills, famed as far as California, Samuel Clemens was ambitious for something more.

But then he ran foul of an anti-dueling statute when he challenged a rival newspaperman, and he and loyal Steve Gillis beat their way in the spring of 1864 to California, where a range of hills stood between them and Nevada jails. Clemens worked briefly as a reporter on the San Francisco *Call,* but it was "fearful drudgery,"

he said, "an awful slavery for a lazy man," so he left regular employment to free-lance for the *Golden Era* and Bret Harte's *Californian*. Then he became San Francisco correspondent for his former paper in Virginia City, until he ran headlong against the law again when Steve Gillis was arrested for barroom brawling and released on bail which Clemens supplied. Then when dapper Steve skipped over the mountains back to Nevada, his protector thought it appropriate to leave also.

This time he took flight to the Sierras, where he stayed on Jackass Hill with Steve Gillis's brother Jim, a teller of tales who was to receive later renown as Bret Harte's "Truthful James." Here, at Angel's Camp, he heard old Ross Coon tell of "The Celebrated Jumping Frog of Calaveras County." Clemens wrote it down, this "villainous, backwoods sketch," in just the rhythm of dialect in which Ross Coon told it, and he sent it east for place in a book of yarns to which Artemus Ward had asked him to contribute. By fortunate mischance it arrived too late for burial in Ward's collection. Instead, it was pirated by the New York *Evening Post* and became an immediate favorite, copied in newspapers all across the country, even in California to give its author prestige there as an eastern writer. For all the good it did him — he made nothing from it.

At just this time, in 1865, the Pacific Steamboat Company began regular passenger service between San Francisco and Honolulu, and Clemens took the trip, paying for it with letters to the *Sacramento Union*, thus setting to final form the pattern which four years later was to establish Mark Twain's reputation with *Innocents Abroad*. These Sandwich Island letters are exuberant, and sometimes vulgar. With him traveled an imaginary, completely irrepressible companion named Mr. Brown, whose sweetheart, he boasted, was so elegant that she picked her nose with a fork. When passengers became seasick, "Brown was there, ever kind and

thoughtful, passing from one to the other and saying, 'That's all right — that's all right you know — it'll clean you out like a jog, and then you won't feel so awful and smell so ridiculous.' "

Mark Twain liked these lovely Pacific islands: "I would rather smell Honolulu at sunset," he wrote, "than the old Police court-room in San Francisco." And he liked the islanders who "always squat on their hams and who knows but they may be the original 'ham sandwiches.' " He liked their customs, especially the "demoralizing *hula hula*" which was forbidden "save at night, with closed doors . . . by permission of the authorities and the payment of ten dollars for the same." Sometimes he became almost lyrical about the beauties of the islands, but when he did, Mr. Brown pulled him up short to remind him that there were also in Honolulu "more 'sentipedes' and scorpions and spiders and mosquitoes and missionaries" than anywhere else in the world.

Clemens had now found the work which suited him best: he could ramble as he pleased and pay his way by being informative and funny. In December 1866 he signed with the *Alta Californian*, the West's most prominent paper, as its "travelling correspondent . . . not stinted as to place, time or direction," who would circle the globe and write letters as he went. The first step in the journey was to New York, the long way around, by boat, and with the ebullient Mr. Brown beside him. The letters written then are more lively than any he had done before, and without the restraints in concession to taste of his later travel accounts. Here he presents the jovial Captain Wakeman, whose tall tales, profanity, and Biblical lore were to live again in Captain Blakely in *Roughing It* and in Captain Stormfield who made a voyage to heaven. There is sentimentality in the account of a runaway couple married at sea, and slapstick aplenty in Mr. Brown's further inelegant concern with seasick passengers, but there is compassion also as Mark Twain

writes of the misery of cholera in Nicaragua, and anger as he snarls at gouging Floridians.

When he arrives in New York, the letters take on fresh vigor, and reveal much which is sometimes said to be characteristic of an older Mark Twain. The "overgrown metropolis" had changed mightily since he had seen it thirteen years before when he was a "pure and sinless sprout." He looked with indignation now on the squalor of her slums where the "criminally, sinfully, wickedly poor" lived amid filth and refuse, victims of their "good, kind-hearted, fat, benevolent" neighbors. His social investigations came to climax when he was arrested for disorderly conduct and spent the night in jail, enraged as he talked with tramps, prostitutes, and former soldiers, pawns at the mercy of society's whim. It is not nec-essary to turn to a later Mark Twain for records of pessimism which damns the whole human race. It is solidly a part of him at thirty.

In New York he saw to the publication of his first book, *The Celebrated Jumping Frog of Calaveras County and Other Sketches*, just as he set out again to continue his wanderings, not around the world, but on an excursion to the Mediterranean and Near East on the steamship *Quaker City*. The letters which he sent back then, to the California paper and also to Horace Greeley's *Tribune* in New York, reached a public ripe for appreciation of his confident assumption that many hallowed shrines of the Old World did not measure to American standards. And such was public response to what he wrote that, when he returned to New York a few months later, the wild mustang of the western plains discovered himself a literary lion, sought by magazines, newspapers, lecture audiences, and publishers.

Caught up by currents of popularity, Samuel Clemens from this time forward was swept from one success to another. He had struck his bonanza, not in silver as he had once dreamed, but in selling

his jocund alter ego in print and from the platform. He met and, after dogged courtship, married Olivia Langdon, daughter of a wealthy New York industrialist. With money advanced by his future father-in-law, he bought a share in a newspaper in Buffalo. The rambler finally would settle down, not permanently as an editor, for that occupation soon palled, but in a magnificent house which royalties and lecture fees would allow him to build in Hartford. He was through, he said, "with literature and all that bosh."

But when *The Innocents Abroad; or, The New Pilgrim's Progress* appeared in 1869, revised from the *Quaker City* letters (with Mr. Brown's offensive commentary, for example, deleted), reviewers found it "fresh, racy, and sparkling as a glass of champagne." The satire was alert, informed, sophisticated, and sidesplittingly funny. The accent was of western humor, but the subject, a favorite among men of good will since the Enlightenment of the century before, spoke of the decay of transatlantic institutions and their shoddiness beside the energetic freshness of the New World. Traveling American innocents haggled through native bazaars, delightedly conscious that every language but their own was ridiculous, and unconscious completely of their own outlandishness. Venice was magnificent, though her boatmen were picturesquely absurd, but the Arno at Florence was darkened by blood shed by the Medici on its shores. The Holy Land was hot and dirty, filled with beggars and larcenous dragomans — when confronted by a boatman at Galilee who demanded exorbitant fare, one of the pilgrims remarked, "No wonder Jesus walked." Because he was clever or because he was by nurture one of them, Clemens touched attitudes shared by many of his countrymen, even to admitting preference for copies of masterpieces because they were brighter than the originals.

To many readers *The Innocents Abroad* remains Clemens's

second-best book, finding place in their affection behind *The Adventures of Huckleberry Finn* and just ahead of, or side by side with, *Life on the Mississippi*. As if anticipating Henry James, it takes a fresh look at the transatlantic world and the stature of Americans when measured against its requirements. Without James's subtlety, conscious art, or depth of penetration, it discovers faults on both sides so that it becomes a book which cosmopolites and chauvinists can equally admire. The hearty and headlong inelegance of the earlier, more carelessly devised travel letters has been pruned from it, and not only because Mark Twain was surrendering to prudish and Victorian notions of propriety. In submitting to the demands of public taste, Clemens was also learning something of the possibilities of converting a casual colloquialism to art.

Roughing It, in 1871, was also greatly successful, suited, said one commentator, "to the wants of the rich, the poor, the sad, the gay," and a sure recipe for laughter. Again it was a book of traveling, the kind that Mark Twain was always to write best, in which one story after another was strung along a journey overland or on water. Every ingredient was here — the tall tale, the straight-faced shocker, melodrama in adventure, insight into raw life among men unrestrained by convention, folklore and animal lore. The effect was of improvisation, for narrative must flow, Clemens later said, as a stream flows, diverted by every boulder, but proceeding briskly, interestingly, on its course.

Such motion did not characterize *The Gilded Age*, published in 1873, which he wrote in collaboration with his Hartford neighbor, Charles Dudley Warner. For the opening chapters Clemens drew on recollections of frontier life to produce situations not unlike those we associate with *Tobacco Road* or *Li'l Abner*, where back-country people dream expansively of fortunes they have neither energy nor ability to acquire. Colonel Beriah Sellers is a hill-town

Mr. Micawber, but drawn from memory of people, even relatives, whom Samuel Clemens had known. Some of the river scenes are beautifully realized. And as the locale shifts to Washington and New York, the novel touches with satirical humor on political corruption, the American jury system, and the mania for speculation, so that it became a best seller and gave title to the age which it reviewed. But artistically it was not a success, for the narrative finally collapses under the weight of plot and counterplot, and is not remembered as one of Mark Twain's best.

Given a story to tell, Clemens was almost always able to tell it well. As raconteur he had come to maturity in *Innocents Abroad*. But the invention of stories did not come easily to him. As he approached forty, he felt written out. He collected miscellaneous writings in *Sketches Old and New* and, with an eye on the market, tried to fit further adventures of the popular Colonel Sellers into a new book which failed to go well but which he published many years later, in 1891, as *The American Claimant*. He labored over a boy's story based on his early life in Hannibal, but that did not go well either.

Finally, at the suggestion of a friend, he recalled his years of steamboating and wrote, with hardly any posturing at all, of "Old Times on the Mississippi" in seven installments for the *Atlantic Monthly* in 1875. Eight years later he was to add thirty-nine chapters to make the book called *Life on the Mississippi*, but the added material, arduously compiled, recaptures little of the charm of these earlier portions. In them the viewpoint is consistently that of a boy bound by the spell of the Mississippi who becomes a pilot and learns her secrets. It is the story of an initiation. Seen from the pilothouse, the river loses much of her glamour; beneath her beauty, painted by sun and shaded by clouds, lurked an implacable menace of snags, hidden reefs, and treacherously changing shores.

The face of the water was a wonderful book, he said, which he was never to forget, and piloting was a profession Clemens loved more than any he followed again: "a pilot in those days was the only unfettered and entirely independent human being that lived on the earth."

On the river he became "personally and familiarly acquainted with about all the different types of human nature to be found in fiction, biography, or history." He never read of or met anyone again without "warm personal interest in him, for the reason that I had known him before — met him on the river." But for all its attention to remembered detail, "Old Times on the Mississippi" was not in strictest sense realistic. Its narrator seldom looked aside to notice people not admitted to the pilothouse, like the sharpers, gamblers, and painted women who plied a profitable trade on Mississippi steamers, but kept his eyes on the river and his mind on the discipline she demanded from men who knew her charm but also her mystery and menace, who were skilled, not only in finding their own way among her dangers, but in guiding others safely through. Thus a reminiscent account becomes more than re-creation of times that are gone and will not return because steamboating, like the whaling of which Melville wrote in *Moby Dick*, was the product of a way of life which was past. It speaks of appearance as opposed to reality, of innocence and experience, of man's duty in a world of perils, and also of a conception of the function of literature.

The Mississippi River appeared triumphantly again in *The Adventures of Tom Sawyer* which in 1876 placed Mark Twain once more at the head of best-seller lists. Probably no more continuingly popular book has ever appeared in the United States. On first reading it seems loose and shambling — as Mark Twain was loose and shambling. Episodes designed "to pleasantly remind adults of what they once were themselves" often remain longer in

memory than the plot of murder and pursuit which must have been intended to hold younger readers. But there is artistry in it also, beyond the artistry of the raconteur who engraved minor realisms about provincial society for all time. Perhaps because he worked long over it, this first independent novel, published when its author was forty, is better constructed than any he was to write again. And its structure reveals levels of meaning which Mark Twain may not have known were there.

The story is divided into three almost exactly equal parts. There are ten chapters in the first part, ten in the second, and thirteen in the climactic third. The first part is separated from the second and the second from the third, each by an interchapter. Within each of the three parts events are detailed carefully, time moves slowly, incident by incident, day by day. In the interchapters time is accelerated, and weeks go by within a few pages. Each of the parts is different from the others in tone, in the kind of adventures in which Tom involves himself, and in the relationship of these adventures to the unifying theme of the whole.

The first ten chapters reveal boys engaged in characteristic play, stealing jam, playing hookey, swapping treasured belongings, until finally they visit a graveyard at midnight and there inadvertently witness a murder. Time has been chronicled exactly, from Friday afternoon to Monday night, but then in the first interchapter, Muff Potter is arrested for the crime which the boys know he did not commit, and two weeks pass. The second part, Chapters 12 through 21, is divided into two major episodes, the Jackson Island adventure and the last day at school. Again time slows down, the boys are again at play, but no longer at simple play of boys among themselves for their own ends: it is directed now against adults, as if in revolt against what the world holds for boys who grow, as Tom has grown, beyond simple innocence to knowledge and, indirectly, participation in evil. After the second interchapter in which sum-

mer days are quickened by the boys' guilty knowledge of Muff's innocence, the plot moves to a cluttered climax.

In the last thirteen chapters the boys begin to act tentatively as adults act. Tom gives evidence in court, he and Huck stalk Injun Joe in a serious, common-sense manner, and they search for treasure which is real and not an imagined product of boyish play. But then Tom shucks off responsibility and goes to a picnic, leaving matter-of-fact Huck to watch for the murderer. And Huck does discover him but only to frighten him into hiding from which he may emerge to strike again. No adult or even adult-like action succeeds in *The Adventures of Tom Sawyer*. In the first part, Aunt Polly is foiled in efforts to have Tom whitewash a fence. In the second part, grownups arrange a funeral for boys who are not dead and the schoolmaster loses his toupee. Now, as the story draws to an end, bumbling adult planning goes astray, and Tom and Becky are lost in the cave for hours before search for them begins. But adult search does not find them, any more than adult efforts do away with the evil which is Injun Joe. Tom's imaginative exploration at the end of a string brings them to safety. Even when adults seal the mouth of the cave, it is not to capture the murderer, but to prevent a recurrence of Tom's kind of adventuring. This notion of the excellence of simple innocence, imaginative and irrepressible, and superior to adult methods of confronting the world, was one to which Mark Twain would often return.

After several years of miscellaneous publication, which included the popular, now forgotten, *Punch, Brothers, Punch and Other Sketches* in 1878 and a second account of European travel, *A Tramp Abroad*, in 1880, Clemens turned to the theme again in *The Prince and the Pauper*, in 1882, but with less success. The account of Tom Canty's adventures in the court of Edward VI was again addressed to boys and girls, tested by readings of the manuscript to the Clemens children and the children of friends,

but it was addressed also to adults as an expression of its author's continuing assurance that, for all its shortcomings, democracy as practiced in the United States was superior to any other manner of living anywhere. It is the kind of melodramatic story which Tom Sawyer might have told, of a poor boy who became heir to a king and of a prince who learned humility through mixing with common men.

"My idea," Clemens told one of his friends, "is to afford a realistic sense of the severity of the laws of that day by inflicting some of their penalties upon the king himself." Poverty which brutalizes and restrictive statutes which force men to thievery are ridiculed, as well as superstition and meaningless ritual. The language of old England, with which Mark Twain had experimented in the surreptitiously printed, mildly ribald *1601, or Conversation as It Was by the Fireside in the Time of the Tudors*, two years before, comes in for a full share of burlesque. When Tom's nose "itcheth cruelly," he asks, "What is the custom and usage of this emergence?" He fills his pockets with nuts and uses the Royal Seal to crack them. When Henry VIII dies and his funeral is delayed to an appropriate ceremonial time in the future, the boy observes, "'Tis strange folly. Will he keep?" Hardly any of the kinds of humor which the public had come to expect from Mark Twain, or of sagacious insight into the frailties of man, is left out of *The Prince and the Pauper*.

In spite of this and largely, Clemens thought, because he had changed to a new publisher, unexperienced in selling copies in great number by subscription, *The Prince and the Pauper* did not do as well commercially as Mark Twain's previous books. So Clemens established his own publishing house and launched it in 1885 with another boy's book which he was careful to link in the public mind to his earlier, encouragingly popular account of young life by the Mississippi by identifying its hero in a subtitle

as "Tom Sawyer's comrade." But *The Adventures of Huckleberry Finn* made no such immediate impression as its predecessor. At Concord in Massachusetts, still the Mecca of genteel New England cultural aspiration, it was banished from the local library as presenting a bad example for youth. Years later, it was blacklisted in Denver, Omaha, and even Brooklyn. When chapters from it appeared in the *Century Magazine,* some readers found it indefensibly coarse, "destitute of a single redeeming quality."

But *The Adventures of Huckleberry Finn* has outlived almost every criticism of those who have spoken against it to become a native classic thrust forward exultantly in the face of any who still dare inquire, "Who reads an American book?" — its health endangered only by a smothering swarm of commentators who threaten to maim it with excessive kind attention. Except perhaps for *Moby Dick*, no American book has recently been opened with more tender explicatory care or by critics to whom we are better prepared to listen. The river on which or beside which the action develops is a great brown god to T. S. Eliot; and Lionel Trilling reminds us of the "subtle, implicit moral meaning of the great river" as he translates Emerson to contemporary idiom by explaining that "Against the money-god stands the river-god, whose comments are silent," that Huck is "the servant of the river-god," and that Mr. Eliot is right in saying "The river is within us."

Other commentators call attention to the social criticism, the satire, the savagery in this book of boy adventures; to its language so cleanly direct and simply natural that reasons for Hemingway's admiration for it come to mind; to its structure which is at one time or to one critic great art, at another fumbling improvisation; to the recurrent imagery, so like what E. M. Forster pointed to in writings of Marcel Proust and called repetition by variation. Its mythic quality is explained as reinforced by elements of popular lore and superstition or by parallels with primitive initiation rites.

The once familiar three-part division of the blackface minstrel show, a genuinely indigenous art form, has been superimposed on *The Adventures of Huckleberry Finn* to reveal instructive similarities. Various interpretations of its theme, some inevitably religious, have been patiently explored. Its endlessness, as if the adventures might have gone on forever, has been persuasively held forth as similar to other distinctively American contrivances which emphasize process rather than product, like the skyscraper, jazz, the comic strip, chewing gum, and *Moby Dick*.

These things are all probably true, if only because attentive readers have discovered them. An encompassing and synthesizing rightness reveals itself now in the casual career of Samuel Clemens who drifted from one occupation to another, managing by accident of birth and qualities which moralists cannot always hold up for emulation to have been at many right places at exactly the right time. His was indeed a pioneer talent, and sometimes so unused to itself that it postured boisterously, almost always ready to break into laughter if response to what was said proved it ridiculous. Its melancholy, even when invaded by the mockery of burlesque, was related to that of home-starved men who sang sad songs on lonesome prairies or rivers, in forests or mountain camps. Its sentimentality was like theirs, ready to retreat to guffaw when detected. The aggressive playfulness which delighted in hoaxes and practical joking changed in almost classic pattern to anger like that of gods — or of simple men — when the joke is turned against them.

Clemens had known backcountry America and the overland push toward great fortunes in the gold-filled, silver-lined West. He had known, better than he learned to know anything else, her great arterial river through which the lifeblood of middle America had once flowed. And he had known men in these places, of all kinds, and then known riches and the company of well-fed, respectable people whom he also recognized as types known before. He

had listened to men talk, boastfully or in anger, had heard their tales and their blandishments, and had learned to speak as they spoke. For his ultimate discovery was linguistic, the creation of a language which was simple, supple, and sustained, in what Richard Chase has called "a joyous exorcism of traditional literary English." No one had ever written like him before. What is more difficult to remember is that no one ever effectively will again because, to say it very simply, his models were not in literature but in life. Even he, when he tried to write something like something he had written before, succeeded only in producing books which were amusing because written in Mark Twain's manner.

The Adventures of Huckleberry Finn is the story of a boy who will not accept the kinds of freedom the world is able to offer, and so flees from them, one after another, to become to many readers a symbol of man's inevitable, restless flight. It is instructive to recall that it appeared in the same year that Clemens's friend William Dean Howells presented in *The Rise of Silas Lapham* another simple protagonist who retreated when confronted by perplexities, and a year before Henry James, who approached maturity through avenues almost completely different from those which Clemens followed, revealed both in *The Princess Casamassima* and *The Bostonians* the struggle of honest young provincials forced to reject promises offered by society. Each played variations on a familiar American theme, which Emerson had expressed, which Whitman approached, and Melville also, and which has reappeared often again. It poses what has been called the inescapable dilemma of democracy — to what degree may each single and separate person live as an unencumbered individual and to what extent must he submit to distortions of personality required by society? If Clemens presented it better than most, by endowing it with qualities of myth interwoven with fantasy, realism, satire, and superstition, it was not because his convictions were different. It was because he

had mastered a language supple enough to reveal the honest observations of an attractive boy and the ambiguous aspirations of many kinds of men whom he came upon, and also the subtly ominous but compelling spirit which in this book is a river.

Huckleberry Finn's solution of the problem of freedom is direct and unworldly: having tested society, he will have none of it, for civilization finally makes culprits of all men. Huck is a simple boy, with little education and great confidence in omens. One measure of his character is its proneness to deceit which, though not always successful, is instinctive, as if it were a trait shared with other wild things, relating him to nature, in opposition to the tradition-grounded, book-learned imaginative deceptions of Tom Sawyer. The dilatory adventures of Huck and his Negro companion, both natural men enslaved, are not unlike the more consciously directed explorations in Faulkner's "The Bear" of Ike McCaslin and his part-Negro, part-Indian guide, if only because they suggest more than can easily be explained.

Young Huck had become something of a hero to the inhabitants of the little river village because of his help to Tom Sawyer in tracking down Injun Joe. He had been adopted by the Widow Douglas, washed, dressed in clean clothes, and sent to school. With Tom he shared the incredible wealth of one dollar a day for each of them derived as income from the treasure they had discovered in *The Adventures of Tom Sawyer*. But Huck is not happy. Tom's make-believe is incomprehensible to him. The religion of retribution which Miss Watson, the widow's sister, teaches makes no sense at all. The religion of love which the widow suggests is better, but he will not commit himself. When his scapegrace father returns and carries Huck across the river to a desolate log house, the boy accepts the abduction with relief because, though he fears his father's beatings and drunken rages, he is freed from restraints of tight clothing, school, and regular hours, and from the preaching

and the puzzling tangle of ideas which confuse village life. But the bondage of life with his father chaffs also, so he steals down the river at night to Jackson Island, where he meets the Negro Jim, Miss Watson's slave, who had run away because his Christian owner was going to sell him.

Thus the first eleven chapters of *The Adventures of Huckleberry Finn* tell of adventures on land, with Huck bewildered or miserable or in flight. The next twenty chapters detail adventures on the river or beside the river, in a pattern of withdrawal and return, as Huck and Jim float with their raft toward what they hope will be freedom for both. On the river or its shores many kinds of men are encountered, most of them evil or stupid or mean: cutthroats, murderers, cheats, liars, swindlers, cowards, slave hunters, dupes and hypocrites of every variety. Even the isolation from society which life on a raft might be thought to afford is violated, for malevolence also intrudes there in grotesque guises. Nor is the movement of the great brown river to be trusted. It carries Jim beyond freedom to capture again by respectable, benevolent people whose conscience is untroubled by human slavery.

The final twelve chapters take place again on land. Tom Sawyer once more appears, filled with romance-bred notions of how Jim might be freed. And Huck joins in the laborious nonsense, for he admires Tom, if he does not understand him — often on the river when confronted with crisis or cleverly, he thought, surmounting difficulties, he wished Tom had been there to aid or commend him. But the boys' make-believe at rescue becomes a travesty, for Miss Watson had granted Jim his freedom — he was no longer a slave. The narrative ends hurriedly, as if embarrassed to linger while loose ends were tied. Huck's father is dead — Jim had known that since the first stage of their journey but in kindness had withheld the knowledge. One threat to Huck's freedom is gone, but another remains, for good people again pity the brave pariah boy

and offer to adopt him. But Huck will not have it: "I can't stand it," he said. "I been there before."

Much has been made of these last chapters, in condemnation or approval. To some readers they certify Clemens's inability to control plot, to others they reveal a compulsive attraction toward elaborate inventions such as Tom Sawyer loved, but to still others they are exactly right, supplying an inevitable rounding out of tale and theme. And much has been made of the development of Huck's character, his initiation, or his disillusionment with the world and its ways, and especially the change in his attitude toward the Negro Jim whom he finally recognizes as a fellow being, more decent and honest than most of the white people who hold him and his kind in slavery. A few find special charm in the assumption that Huck does not develop in any fundamental sense at all, because as a child of nature he is changeless. But to all, it is Huck and his view of the world which secure for this book its high place among American writings.

For one of the things to notice about *The Adventures of Huckleberry Finn* is that Mark Twain is not the narrator. Huck makes that plain in the first paragraph: Mr. Mark Twain had written of him in *The Adventures of Tom Sawyer*, he said, but this would be his own story. And the first-person narrative which follows allows Huck to misspell and mispronounce words in a manner which could delight admirers of Mark Twain, and to act sometimes in a manner which he thought would have delighted Tom Sawyer, but it is his voice which speaks, authentically and without posturing. Sometimes Mark Twain's accents are heard, as compellingly humorous as ever, tempting attention away from the boy who, with no humor at all, struggles to make himself understood. But Huck is finally the better witness, infinitely better than Tom Sawyer whose vision is blurred by boyish trickery very different from Huck's protective deceit.

Boyish Tom, however, seems to have been Mark Twain's favorite. He wrote of him again in *Tom Sawyer Abroad* in 1894 and in *Tom Sawyer Detective* in 1896, contrived books, imitative of earlier successes, and crowded with imagined adventure rather than experience. Yet, with boyhood behind him, even Tom was not to be envied. Clemens once thought of writing of the two boys as adults who return to their river village. "Huck comes back sixty years old, from nobody knows where — and crazy." He imagines himself a boy again and watches everyone who passes to find the face of one of his boyhood friends. Then Tom returns, from years of "wandering in the world," and they talk of old times. "Both are desolate, life has been a failure, all that was lovable, all that was beautiful was under the sod."

But if old times in backcountry America were idyllically best, older times in Europe certainly were not. Far too many of his countrymen, Clemens thought, were beguiled by romantic notions popularized by Sir Walter Scott, which made overgrown Tom Sawyers of them all. Scott was "so juvenile, so artificial, so shoddy," not once "recognizably sincere and in earnest." His characters were "bloodless shams," "milk-and-water humbugs," "squalid shadows." Nor were American romancers, bred under Scott's influence, appreciably better. Among the most persistently anthologized of Clemens's short pieces is the humorously perceptive dissection of "Fenimore Cooper's Literary Offenses" in which he finds that "in the restricted space of two-thirds of a page, Cooper has scored 114 offenses against literary art out of a possible 115." He speaks of Cooper's "crass stupidities," his lack of attention to detail, and his curious box of stage properties which contained such hackneyed devices as the broken twig: "It is a restful chapter in any book of his when somebody doesn't step on a twig and alarm all the reds and whites for two hundred yards around. . . . In fact, the Leatherstocking Series ought to have been called the Broken

Twig Series." Surely, Clemens reasoned, history could be presented without such twaddle.

So Clemens wrote of the adventures of a sturdy, practical nineteenth-century mechanic who is knocked unconscious by a blow on the head and awakes to find himself under a tree near Camelot, amid a landscape "as lovely as a dream and as lonesome as Sunday." But *The Connecticut Yankee in King Arthur's Court*, published in 1889, was double-edged in satirical intention. The Yankee proves himself a better man than the magician Merlin and he overcomes the best of knights in single or multiple combat. He provides what he called "a new deal" for downtrodden common people, transforming Arthur's England into a technically efficient going concern in which gunpowder and mechanical skills triumph over superstition, injustice, and oppression. But "this Yankee of mine," explained Clemens, "is a perfect ignoramus; he is boss of a machine shop, he can build a locomotive or a Colt's revolver, he can put up and run a telegraph line, but he's an ignoramus nevertheless."

The Connecticut Yankee has been called Mark Twain's finest possibility, combining satire, the tall tale, humor, democracy, religion, and the damned human race. Loosely picaresque and brightly anecdotal, it was an attempt, Clemens explained, "to imagine and after a fashion set forth, the hard condition of life for the laboring and defenseless poor in bygone times in England, and incidentally contrast those conditions with those under which civil and ecclesiastical pets of privilege and high fortune lived in those times." But what finally emerges from beneath the contrast between Yankee ingenuity and medieval superstition is the portrait of an American. He is unlearned, with "neither the refinement nor the weakness of a college education," but quick-witted and completely, even devastatingly successful. Consciously created or not, it is the image of Samuel Clemens and of many of his

friends. And it explains something of the nature of the literature which he and his fellows produced.

Meanwhile Clemens had thought for years that he might write a comic story about Siamese twins, one of whom was good, the other a rake, imagining that sidesplitting situations could result when, for example, the rake drank to excess and the teetotaler twin became intoxicated. Perhaps no idea was more grotesquely unfavorable for fiction, and Clemens never developed it fully, partly because, as he said, "A man who is not born with the novel-writing gift has a troublesome time of it when he tries to write a novel. . . . He has no clear idea of his story; in fact he has no story. He has merely some people in his mind, and an incident or two, also a locality . . . and he trusts that he can plunge those people into those incidents with interesting results."

When he did put shreds of this tale together in *Those Extraordinary Twins*, he pretended jocosely to reveal something of his casual literary method, particularly in dealing with characters who became lost amid the intricacies of plot. One female character named Rowena, for example, began splendidly but failed to keep up: "I must simply give her the grand bounce," he said. "It grieved me to do it, for after associating with her so much I had come to kind of like her after a fashion, notwithstanding she was such an ass, and said such stupid, irritating things, and was so nauseatingly sentimental." So he sent her "out into the back yard after supper to see the fireworks," and "she fell down a well and got drowned." The method seemed perhaps abrupt, "but I thought maybe the reader wouldn't notice it, because I changed the subject right away to something else. Anyway it loosened Rowena up from where she was stuck and got her out of the way, and that was the main thing."

Successful once, he resolved to try the stratagem again with two boys who were no longer useful ("they went out one night to stone a cat and fell down the well and got drowned") and with

two supernumerary old ladies ("they went out one night to visit the sick and fell down a well and got drowned"). "I was going to drown some of the others, but I gave up the idea, partly because I believed that if I kept it up I would attract attention, and perhaps sympathy with those people, and partly because it was not a large well and would not hold any more anyway."

This was pure Mark Twain, in mood and language which many people liked best. Part of the fun was that what he said was so true or seemed so true in revelation of the shambling way he really wrote or liked to have people think he wrote stories. And the laugh was on him, or seemed to be, at the same time that it mocked conventional or sentimental writers who had no convenient wells in their back yards. Almost everybody agreed that Mark Twain made most sense when he was funniest. He could double people over with laughter as he pointed to their shortcomings or his own or those of people not quite so clever as they. The laughter was cleansing, but quieting also, for surely such amusing peccadilloes needed no correction.

Those Extraordinary Twins appeared in 1894 as an appendix to *The Tragedy of Pudd'nhead Wilson*, a better story which unaccountably had grown from it. Using the same device of the changeling which had provided the plot for *The Prince and the Pauper*, he told now of two children born on the same day in the Driscoll home at Dawson's Landing, one the son of the white master of the house, the other of a mulatto slave named Roxana, who switched the babies in their cradles so that her tainted son was brought up as Thomas à Becket Driscoll, heir to estates, while Tom, the white boy, became a slave. The bogus Tom grew to be a wastrel, a thief, and finally a murderer. When his mother threatened to expose him if he did not change his ways, he sold her to a slave trader.

The mulatto Roxana dominates the book, sentimentally per-

haps, but illustrating again qualities of nobility like those which Huck discovered in the Negro Jim. But her attitudes on race are ambiguous and have puzzled people who would relate them to Huck's attitude or Jim's. When her son proved himself in every respect bad, she told him, "It's de nigger in you, dat's what it is. Thirty-one parts o' you is white, en only one part nigger, en dat po' little one part is yo' soul. 'Taint wuth savin', 'taint wuth totin' out in a shovel en throwin' in de gutter." Perhaps it is a mistake to expect consistency in a writer like Clemens. Or perhaps the greater mistake is to think that any one book of his can be used as commentary on any other.

Potentially more significant is the title character, a lawyer fond of philosophical maxims, but considered queer, a Pudd'nhead, by the rest of the community because he fails to conform to village standards. Among his strange hobbies is that of taking fingerprints, and he had years before made prints of the baby boys before they were changed about. When the trial for the murder which the bogus Tom had committed is held and Italian twins (the remnant of the Siamese twin idea) are blamed for it because they have the misfortune of being foreigners and strangers in the village, Pudd'nhead defends them, dramatically revealing by means of his prints that the true murderer is Roxana's villainous son.

The Tragedy of Pudd'nhead Wilson is filled with familiar failings, false starts, and rambling excursions. The title makes us wonder why it is Pudd'nhead's tragedy. But it contains excellencies also, of a kind which Sherwood Anderson was to use in writing about village people, and which have earned for it a reputation as "the most extraordinary book in American literature," filled with intolerable insights into evil. Even distorted by drollery, it penetrates toward recognition of social ills not unlike those which William Faulkner was later to probe. Beneath the burlesque which peoples the sleepy village of Dawson's Landing with representa-

tives of decayed gentry bearing such exuberant names as Percy Northumberland Driscoll and Cecil Burleigh Essex runs a vein of satire which allows recognition of these people as ancestors of the Sartorises and Compsons. Pudd'nhead himself might have sat as model for Faulkner's Gavin Stevens, who comments on tradition-ridden life in Yoknapatawpha County. The octoroon who masquerades as white can be thought of as a tentative foreshadowing of Joe Christmas in *Light in August* or Sutpen's half-caste son in *Absalom, Absalom!*

Its failure is literary, the failure of words, not of ideas. Mark Twain is telling a story according to a familiar pattern, incident strung on incident as if they might go on forever. Humor, pathos, sentiment, anger, and burlesque rub shoulders with intimacy bred of long acquaintance. *Pudd'nhead Wilson* is serious in intention, for all its belly-laughs and tears. It faces up to problems made by the venality of man. Seldom is it more plainly evident that Mark Twain's eyes rarely twinkle when he laughs. A social conscience here is plainly showing. Scorn looks boldly out from behind the burlesque. But the words do not come true, as Huck's words did or as Clemens's did when he remembered apprentice days on the river. He is saying what he wants to say, but in accents which ring false because they speak now as people expected him to speak.

Perhaps it is even possible to suppose that Mark Twain, who was responsible for so much of Clemens's incomparable contemporary success, became finally an encumbrance. As Stephen Crane once said, two hundred pages is a very long stretch in which to be funny. And the stretch is more enervating when the humorist understands that what he writes about is not of itself funny, but only seems so because of the way he writes about it. Man was more likely than not to be mean and do wrong — this even Huck knew, who was not humorous at all. Clemens seems to have known it also, and for a long time.

But Clemens had never kept his observations on the venality of man completely in focus, not even in *The Adventures of Huckleberry Finn*. Whether his seasoning of humor and relaxed excursions into anecdote are uniformly successful or not, they do reveal a distinctively practical approach to literature. I can teach anyone to write a successful story, he once advised a literary friend. All that needs to be done is catch the reader's attention with the first sentence and hold it by whatever means are possible to the end. The story flows, he said, as a stream flows, and the storyteller's responsibility is to pilot the reader in safety and comfort through its often meandering channel.

During the twenty years between 1875 and 1894 Samuel Clemens was happiest, and wealthiest, and he wrote his best books. He lived then in luxury among a group of well-to-do litterateurs in Hartford. He lectured, assumed an occasional editorial commitment, and sought attractive books for distribution by his publishing house. His income was breathtaking, probably mounting more than once to one hundred thousand dollars a year. But money went as fast as it came, especially in speculative enterprises like the typesetting machine into which he poured much of his earnings. He dreamed like Colonel Sellers of making millions, as many of his contemporaries did, but by the mid 1890's he was bankrupt. A world tour then brought him increased fame and respect, produced *Following the Equator* in 1897, paid his debts, and provided new financial security. But at sixty, his effective literary career could be considered finished.

While resident in Europe he completed the writing of *Personal Recollections of Joan of Arc*, an account so seriously intended as the expression of a lifelong admiration that it was published in 1896 without Clemens's familiar pseudonym for fear that readers might expect another comic book from Mark Twain and laugh.

The innocent faith of the Maid of Orleans represented a quality pitiably absent from modern life. She seemed "easily and by far the most extraordinary person the human race has ever produced." Untrained and without experience, she had within herself a capacity for goodness so pure and successful that it was condemned as heresy by men whom the world named good. But, hampered perhaps by the necessity of keeping close to what he had learned through years of reading of Joan's history, Clemens did not tell her story well, and few readers have agreed with him that it made his best book.

Grief and increasing bitterness had begun to close in upon him, to darken the rest of his life. His daughter Susie died suddenly while her parents were abroad, Mrs. Clemens was distressingly ill for years and then died, and his youngest daughter died suddenly one Christmas Eve. During the fifteen years which preceded his own death in 1910, Clemens lashed out often in anger at a world which had wounded him or reminisced with increasing compulsion on a world which was gone. He could not bear to return to Hartford where he had been happily successful, but moved restlessly from place to place, from residence in New York, to Florence in Italy, to Bermuda for his health, and finally to Stormfield in rural Connecticut, writing furiously at more projects than he could ever complete.

Readers who found Tom Sawyer silly or Huck Finn finally a profitless model were moved to wry approval of *The Man That Corrupted Hadleyburg* which in 1900 presented Clemens's most trenchant testimony to the fundamental dishonesty of man. Piercing the shell of respectability which traditionally had made each small town seem inhabited by kindly hearts and gentle people, he demonstrated how easily even prominently moral citizens could be led beyond temptation when confronted with opportunity to acquire wealth dishonestly but undetected. None were exempt,

for every contest was rigged. No more astringent or cynical condemnation of contemporary mores had been issued by an American; even Stephen Crane's *Maggie* eight years before and Theodore Dreiser's *Sister Carrie* of the same year seem tempered with sentiments which Clemens could no longer feel. A year later, in *A Person Sitting in Darkness*, he struck savagely at the militant morality of missionaries, and in *King Leopold's Soliloquy*, in 1905, scornfully denounced pious exploitation of underdeveloped countries. *Extracts from Adam's Diary* in 1904 and *Eve's Diary* in 1906 were whimsical accounts of the dependence of even the first man on the superior management of women, and spoke feelingly by indirection of the loneliness of life without connubial and familial affection.

In 1906 he began to dictate his autobiography, reviewing, often without any defense of humor, incidents and personalities remembered from his rambling career. Some parts were so forthright that he thought they should not be published for a century after his death, but other parts were sent off for immediate serialization in the *North American Review*. Selected portions have been put together for *Mark Twain's Autobiography* in 1924, *Mark Twain in Eruption* in 1940, and *The Autobiography of Mark Twain* in 1959, each adding its effective extension to the image of a favorite American, who grumbled and growled, who smoked too much and cadged Scotch whiskey from his wealthy friends, but who had been places and who was known and loved all over the world.

In 1906 he also issued privately and anonymously what he called his "wicked book," *What Is Man?* which contains his most astringent diagnosis of man as a mechanism, the plaything of chance, his brain "so constructed that it can originate nothing." Man is a chameleon who "by the law of his nature . . . takes on the color of the place of his resort. The influences about him create his preferences, his aversions, his politics, his taste, his morality, his reli-

gion." All that he knows, all that he does, is determined by one inexorable law: "From his cradle to his grave a man never does a single thing which has any first and foremost object but one — to secure peace of mind, spiritual comfort, for himself." He is what he is, and nothing will change him. Self-seeking, self-admiring, he babbles of free will and love and compassion, which are fictions made to ensure his satisfaction with himself. "Whenever you read of a self-sacrificing act or hear of one, or of a duty done for duty's sake, take it to pieces and look for the real motive. It's always there."

The book is not wicked, but it is tired. Its words speak forthrightly, despairingly, echoing the words of other men who testified to man's slavery to forces beyond himself. They are palliative as well as condemnatory, as if their writer were explaining to himself as much as to other men why it was necessary for all men to do what he and they perforce had done. Resolution is not lacking, nor anger. On its level, the book argues well. It presents its case. What is no longer there is the power of the inevitable word which is in so intimate a relation to the thing of which it speaks that meaning spills over to intimations which ordinary words can never reach. Once Clemens's words had clung thus close to things, but now they gestured and had less to say.

Six months before his death Clemens released an *Extract from Captain Stormfield's Visit to Heaven*, a favorite tale over which he had been puttering for many years. In it almost every contrivance of humor, sentiment, or dissection of human frailty that Mark Twain had ever used was expended again on the adventures of a crusty, matter-of-fact mariner who went flashing through the air like a bird toward paradise, racing a comet on the way as steamboat pilots used to race on the Mississippi. He has difficulty in finding wings that fit or a harp that suits him. He seeks long before finding the proper resting place for people from a planet so

little valued by angels that they call it the Wart. He has trouble conversing with people who speak ridiculous languages, tumbles terribly in learning to fly, is surprised to find Jews and Moslems in heaven, and pleased that Shakespeare is placed "away down there below shoe-makers and horse-dealers and knife-grinders" to make room for an unknown tailor from Tennessee who "wrote poetry that Homer and Shakespeare couldn't begin to come up to; but nobody would print it, nobody read it but his neighbors, and they laughed at it." Recognition of wisdom masked by such burlesque is usually considered the test of a true admirer of Mark Twain.

But no subtlety of interpretation is required for recognition of the bleak despair of Clemens's posthumous *The Mysterious Stranger*. The scene is Austria in 1590, where in the village of Eseldorf, a paradise for play like that which Tom and Huck had known, three boys are joined by a visiting angel, namesake and nephew of the fallen Satan. He entertains them with miracles, making little creatures of clay, breathing life into them, and then mashing them down as if they were flies. It seems cruel to the boys, but Satan explains that it was not cruel, only capricious and, as far as man could understand, ordained. Crippled by moral sense, in bondage to circumstance, his vision distorted by illusion, man pampers himself with ideals which exist only when he imagines them. What an ass he is! How hysterically mad are his expectations: "No sane man can be happy, for to him life is real, and he sees what a fearful thing it is," for "there is no God, no universe, no human race, no earthly life, no heaven, no hell. It is all a dream — a grotesque and foolish dream. Nothing exists," said the angel, "but you. And you are but a *thought* — a vagrant thought, a useless thought, a homeless thought, wandering forlorn among the empty eternities."

Nothing remains of the Widow Douglas's reliance on the religion of love or Huck's possibility of escape from the world through

flight. Again Clemens speaks, as he had in 1885, of ideas which unsettled many people of his time, but now others voiced them better than he, for some magic of language has disappeared from these late sputtering insights of anger and despair. The angel Satan speaks, but the words are Clemens's, in reprimand as much to himself as to those who read him: "You have a mongrel sense of humor, nothing more," he charged; "you see the comic side of a thousand low-grade and trivial things — broad incongruities, mainly; grotesqueries, absurdities, evokers of the horse-laugh." But the "ten thousand high-grade comicalities" made by the juvenilities of man are sealed from your dull visions. "Will a day come when the race will detect these juvenilities and laugh at them — and by laughing destroy them?" In a perfect world there is no room for laughter, but this world is not perfect, and man in his poverty "has unquestionably one really effective weapon — laughter. Power, money, persuasion, supplication, persecution — these can lift at a colossal humbug — push it a little — weaken it a little, century by century; but only laughter can blow it to rags and atoms at a blast."

"Humor," Mark Twain once wrote when in another mood, "is only a fragrance, a decoration." If it is really to succeed in survival, it must surreptitiously teach and preach. Perhaps that is why so sober an admirer as James T. Farrell sees in Huck and Tom "two accusing fingers pointing down the decades of America's history," relentlessly questioning why it is in America, or perhaps anywhere else, that a man so rarely becomes what the boy gave promise of becoming. Samuel Clemens did see the world as a boy sees it, in its infinitude of possibilities for freedom and fun and in its darkened depths of disillusionment. And, like a boy, when embarrassed he laughed; when tentatively serious he laughed first, so that the responding laugh could be with, not at, him; even in tantrum, he seemed somehow comic, an object which in brighter spirits he

43

might have ridiculed. "From a boyhood idyll of the good life to a boy's criticism of that life," says Wright Morris in accusation, "is the natural range and habitat of the American mind." Mark Twain's charm of innocence did isolate him from maturity. What he achieved artlessly so well that he invented a theory of storytelling art to explain it was received with riotous applause by his countrymen. With so natural a talent why should he then not attempt more? Clemens's inability to respond to that question explains much of Mark Twain and the milieu which made him possible. But it fails to explain all, or even what is most important.

Samuel Clemens created or became Mark Twain who boundlessly created laughter, but he was more than a buffoon. As comic realist he applies for place beside Laurence Sterne, Dickens, Joyce, Faulkner, and Camus, for his eyes like theirs have seen beyond locality to qualities which men universally, sometimes shamefully, share. To remember him only as a creator of boyhood adventure or as a relic of an American frontier or the voice of native idiosyncrasy is to do him disservice. His accomplishment finally contradicts his thinking, thus certifying his literary achievement. Much that is excellent in American literature *did* begin with him, and Lionel Trilling is correct when he says "that almost every contemporary American writer who deals conscientiously with the problems and possibilities of prose must feel, directly or indirectly, the influence of . . . [his] style which escapes the fixity of the printed page, that sounds in our ears with the immediacy of the heard voice, the very voice of unpretentious truth."

But he was anticipated also, ten years before his first triumphant entry to public notice, by another native observer who admitted men "victims of illusion" and life "a succession of dreams." Samuel Clemens, Mississippi pilot, had not yet become Mark Twain but Emerson had someone much like him in mind when he described "a humorist who in a good deal of rattle had a grain or two of

sense. He shocked the company by maintaining that the attributes of God were two, — power and risibility, and that it was the duty of every pious man to keep up the comedy."

Perhaps it was a basic lack of piety in the sense of dedication to the demands of literature ("and all that bosh") which deprived Samuel Clemens of an ability consistently to keep up the comedy. Laughter is not joy, funny fellows are notoriously prone to tears, and the comic view has never sustained man's highest vision of himself or his possibilities because, as Baudelaire once said, the comic is imitation, not creation. But his countrymen seldom chide Mark Twain for what he is not; what he was is good enough, and plenty. It is probably true that the sense of the comic, the ability to laugh, is in him who laughs, and not in the object which excites his laughter. If the thousand low-grade and trivial things which quickened mirth among his countrymen were more often displayed than Samuel Clemens's occasional genuine and high-grade comicalities, the fault was not his alone, and he is not to be blamed for his anger, except that it came too late, when his words were tired. He shocked his countrymen by explaining what they were, and they laughed. Their continuing laughter measures his genius and their own, and the limitations they have shared together.

⤝ Selected Bibliography

THE most complete edition is *Mark Twain's Works*, 37 volumes (New York: Harper, 1929). See also Merle Johnson, *A Bibliography of Mark Twain* (New York: Harper, 1935), and E. H. Long, *Mark Twain Handbook* (New York: Hendricks House, 1957), which list important critical articles.

Principle Writings of Mark Twain

The Innocents Abroad; or, The New Pilgrim's Progress. Hartford, Conn.: American Publishing Co., 1869.

Roughing It. Hartford, Conn.: American Publishing Co., 1872.

The Gilded Age (with C. D. Warner). Hartford, Conn.: American Publishing Co., 1874.

The Adventures of Tom Sawyer. Hartford, Conn.: American Publishing Co., 1876.

A Tramp Abroad. Hartford, Conn.: American Publishing Co., 1880.

The Prince and the Pauper. Boston: Osgood, 1882.

Life on the Mississippi. Boston: Osgood, 1883.

The Adventures of Huckleberry Finn. New York: Webster, 1885.

A Connecticut Yankee in King Arthur's Court. New York: Webster, 1889.

The Tragedy of Pudd'nhead Wilson. Hartford, Conn.: American Publishing Co., 1894.

Personal Recollections of Joan of Arc. New York: Harper, 1896.

Following the Equator. Hartford, Conn.: American Publishing Co., 1897.

The Man That Corrupted Hadleyburg and Other Stories and Essays. New York: Harper, 1900.

Extract from Captain Stormfield's Visit to Heaven. New York: Harper, 1909.

The Mysterious Stranger. New York: Harper, 1916.

Mark Twain's Autobiography, edited by A. B. Paine. New York: Harper, 1924.

Mark Twain's Letters from the Sandwich Islands, edited by G. Ezra Dane. Palo Alto, Calif.: Stanford University Press, 1938.

Mark Twain's Travels with Mr. Brown, edited by G. Ezra Dane. New York: Knopf, 1940.

Mark Twain in Eruption, edited by Bernard De Voto. New York: Harper, 1940.

The Autobiography of Mark Twain, edited by Charles Neider. New York: Harper, 1959.

Mark Twain-Howells Letters, edited by H. N. Smith and W. M. Gibson. Cambridge, Mass.: Belknap Press, 1960.

Current American Reprints

The Modern Classics Series published by Harper and Brothers includes reprints of *Innocents Abroad, Tom Sawyer, The Prince and the Pauper, Huckleberry Finn,* and *The Connecticut Yankee* ($1.25 each). *Huckleberry Finn* and *The Mysterious Stranger* are in *The Portable Mark Twain,* edited by Bernard De Voto (New York: Viking. $1.45).

The Adventures of Huckleberry Finn. New York: Pocket Books. $.35. New York: Rinehart Reprint Series. $.65. Boston: Riverside (Houghton Mifflin). $.80. New York: Signet (New American Library). $.50.

The Adventures of Tom Sawyer. New York: Pocket Books. $.35. New York: Signet. $.50.

Complete Short Stories of Mark Twain, edited by Charles Neider. New York: Bantam. $.75.

A Connecticut Yankee in King Arthur's Court. New York: Modern Library (Random House). $1.95. New York: Washington Square Press. $.35.

Life on the Mississippi. New York: Bantam. $.50.

Mark Twain: A Modern Anthology, edited by Edmund Fuller. New York: Dell. $.50.

Pudd'nhead Wilson. New York: Bantam. $.35. New York: Evergreen (Grove). $1.45.

Roughing It. New York: Rinehart Reprint Series. $.95.

Tom Sawyer and Huckleberry Finn. New York: Modern Library. $2.95.

Critical and Biographical Studies

Andrews, Kenneth R. *Nook Farm: Mark Twain's Hartford Circle.* Cambridge, Mass.: Harvard University Press, 1950.

Asselineau, Roger. *The Literary Reputation of Mark Twain.* Paris: Libraire Marcel Didier, 1954.

Bellamy, Gladys C. *Mark Twain as a Literary Artist.* Norman: University of Oklahoma Press, 1950.

Benson, Ivan. *Mark Twain's Western Years.* Palo Alto, Calif.: Stanford University Press, 1938.

Blair, Walter. *Mark Twain and Huck Finn.* Berkeley: University of California Press, 1960.

Branch, Edgar M. *The Literary Apprenticeship of Mark Twain.* Urbana: University of Illinois Press, 1950.

Brashear, M. M. *Mark Twain, Son of Missouri.* Chapel Hill: University of North Carolina Press, 1934.

47

Brooks, Van Wyck. *The Ordeal of Mark Twain*. Revised edition. New York: Dutton, 1933.

Clemens, Clara. *My Father, Mark Twain*. New York: Harper, 1931.

De Voto, Bernard. *Mark Twain at Work*. Cambridge, Mass.: Harvard University Press, 1942.

————. *Mark Twain's America*. Boston: Little, Brown, 1935.

Eliot, T. S. Introduction to *The Adventures of Huckleberry Finn*. New York: Chanticleer Press, 1950.

Ferguson, J. DeLancey. *Mark Twain: Man and Legend*. Indianapolis: Bobbs Merrill, 1943.

Howells, William Dean. *My Mark Twain*. New York: Harper, 1910.

Liljegren, S. B. *The Revolt against Romanticism in American Literature as Evidenced in the Works of S. L. Clemens*. Upsala: Lundequistska Bokhandeln, 1945.

Lynn, Kenneth S. *Mark Twain and Southwestern Humor*. Boston: Atlantic-Little Brown, 1960.

Paine, Albert Bigelow. *Mark Twain: A Biography*. Revised edition in 2 volumes. New York: Harper, 1935.

Schönemann, Friedrich. *Mark Twain als literarische Persönlichkeit*. Berlin: Verlag der Frommanschen Buchhandlung, Walter Biedermann, 1925.

Scott, Arthur L., ed. *Mark Twain: Selected Criticism*. Dallas: Southern Methodist University Press, 1955.

Trilling, Lionel. Introduction to *The Adventures of Huckleberry Finn*. New York: Rinehart, 1948.

Wagenknecht, Edward. *Mark Twain: The Man and His Work*. New Haven: Yale University Press, 1935.

Wecter, Dixon. *Sam Clemens of Hannibal*. Boston: Houghton Mifflin, 1952.

UNIVERSITY OF MINNESOTA
PAMPHLETS ON AMERICAN WRITERS

William Van O'Connor, Allen Tate, and
Robert Penn Warren, editors

Willard Thorp, Karl Shapiro, and Philip Rahv, advisers

1. **ERNEST HEMINGWAY** by Philip Young

2. **ROBERT FROST** by Lawrance Thompson

3. **WILLIAM FAULKNER** by William Van O'Connor

4. **HENRY JAMES** by Leon Edel

5. **MARK TWAIN** by Lewis Leary

6. **THOMAS WOLFE** by C. Hugh Holman

EACH PAMPHLET, 65 CENTS

UNIVERSITY OF MINNESOTA PRESS, Minneapolis 14
Minnesota, U.S.A.